Who Is Billie Jean King?

by Sarah Fabiny

illustrated by Dede Putra

Penguin Workshop

To my dad—thank you for putting
a tennis racket in my hands—SF

PENGUIN WORKSHOP
An imprint of Penguin Random House LLC, New York

First published in the United States of America by Penguin Workshop,
an imprint of Penguin Random House LLC, New York, 2024

Visit us online at penguinrandomhouse.com.

Library of Congress Cataloging-in-Publication Data is available.

Printed in the United States of America

ISBN 9780593519172 (paperback)   10 9 8 7 6 5 4 3 2 1 CJKW
ISBN 9780593519189 (library binding)   10 9 8 7 6 5 4 3 2 1 CJKW

Contents

Who Is Billie Jean King?

Twenty-nine-year-old Billie Jean King could hardly hear herself think as she waited in the locker room for the tennis match to start. More than thirty thousand spectators filled the Astrodome in Houston, Texas. They were shouting and whistling and stomping their feet. Every other tennis match that Billie Jean had played required that the audience be quiet and respectful. But this match on September 20, 1973, was different. It wasn't a match in an official tennis tournament. Billie Jean wasn't trying to win a trophy. It was a tennis match called the Battle of the Sexes. Ninety million people around the world were watching it on TV. And Billie Jean was playing to prove to her opponent, fifty-five-year-old Bobby Riggs, and the entire world that women were just as good at tennis as men!

At most tournaments, Billie Jean just walked from the locker room out onto the tennis court. But tonight, she was carried out onto the court on a fancy chair called a litter, the kind of chair that Queen Cleopatra, a ruler of ancient Egypt, might have used. The litter was covered in plastic gems and ostrich feathers, and it was carried by four men dressed in costumes meant to look like ancient Egyptians. As Billie Jean made her way to the tennis court, cameras flashed, a band played, and a famous sports announcer named Howard Cosell introduced her to the crowd. But at this point in her career, Billie Jean King didn't really need an introduction. She was a top tennis player who was known for demanding big changes to the game of tennis.

Bobby Riggs, Billie Jean's current opponent, had recently beaten thirty-year-old Margaret Court, Billie Jean's main rival, in a tennis match.

And he was sure he would beat Billie Jean just as easily. He believed that women weren't as good as men at playing tennis—or at doing anything. His entrance to the tennis court was just as showy as Billie Jean's. He was in a rickshaw that was pulled by several young women. (A rickshaw is a chair on two large wheels that is pulled by a person or animal.)

Billie Jean had been practicing for this match for months. A lot was on the line. If she lost,

people would agree with Bobby Riggs that women were not as good as men. If she won, the world might start to believe that women deserved to be respected and have the same rights as men.

Even though there was a lot riding on the match, Billie Jean felt calm and confident. She stepped down from the litter onto the tennis court. Showtime was over. It was time to play tennis.

CHAPTER 1
What's Tennis?

Billie Jean Moffitt was born on November 22, 1943, in Long Beach, California, a city that's about a half-hour drive south of Los Angeles.

Her father, Bill, was a firefighter, and her mother, Betty, was a homemaker. Billie Jean was the first child born to Betty and Bill Moffitt. Her brother, Randy, was born five years later.

Betty had thought she would name their daughter Michelle Louise. But Bill was called to serve in World War II before the baby was born. So in case Bill didn't come back from the war, Betty decided that she should name their baby girl after him.

The Moffitts were a middle-class and an athletic family. Bill was a talented basketball player, and he had been offered a tryout for what is now a National Basketball Association (NBA) team. Betty was an excellent swimmer and a fast runner. Randy loved baseball and had announced to his family that he wanted to be a professional athlete. (He grew up to be a Major League Baseball [MLB] pitcher and played for the San Francisco Giants, Houston Astros, and

Toronto Blue Jays.) When she was just four years old, Billie Jean and her dad started playing catch with a rubber baseball in the backyard.

As she grew older, Billie Jean loved playing softball and football with the boys in the neighborhood. She even dreamed of playing professional football for the Green Bay Packers one day.

Billie Jean was a good athlete, and she did well in any sport she tried. Like her brother, she wanted to be a professional athlete when she grew up. But her parents were worried that their daughter would get hurt if she kept playing softball and football. And Billie Jean's mother also felt that those sports weren't very "ladylike." She thought Billie Jean should switch to a sport that wasn't so rough. She suggested that Billie Jean try golf or swimming. Billie Jean felt that golf was too slow, and she was actually too afraid of the water to try swimming.

Billie Jean also liked playing sports because it was a way for her to not feel so shy and awkward at school. She was bigger than all the girls, and even some of the boys, in her class.

Because of that, she hated having to stand up in front of the class and give reports. But when Billie Jean was playing sports, her size was an advantage, and she forgot all about her insecurities.

One day in 1954, when Billie Jean was in the fifth grade, a friend named Susan Williams asked her if she wanted to play tennis. "What's tennis?" Billie Jean replied. Susan explained what the game was, and Billie Jean agreed to join Susan at the country club her family belonged to. Although Billie Jean didn't play very well, she loved that in tennis you could run,

jump, and hit a ball—the things that Billie Jean loved doing the most. When she got home, she asked her dad which sport he thought would be best for a girl to play long-term. "Well," he said, "there's swimming, golf, and tennis." She was happy to hear that tennis was a sport that her parents would let her continue to play.

An Introduction to Tennis

Tennis is played on a rectangular court with a net that divides the court into two halves. Players use rackets to hit a ball back and forth over the net. The goal of the game is to hit the ball over the net into the opponent's half of the court so that the opponent is unable to return the ball. Tennis matches are either singles, with just two players; or doubles, with four players (two teams of two players each).

Scoring in tennis is based on points, games, and sets. Zero points is a score of 0 (also called *love*). One point is a score of 15, two points is 30, and three points is 40. When someone wins a point after they reach 40, they win the game! The first player to win six games wins a set. Women's matches are usually two to three sets, and men's matches are usually three to five sets.

Major Walter Clopton Wingfield from Great Britain published the first book of tennis rules in 1873. The first tennis championship took place four years later. It was held in a part of London, England, called Wimbledon. Now, the United Kingdom, Australia, France, and the United States each hold a major international tennis tournament each year. Together, the four tournaments are known as the Grand Slams. The Wimbledon tournament is the oldest Grand Slam event.

Clyde Walker

A few weeks later, Billie Jean and Susan went to the public tennis courts in Long Beach. A tennis coach named Clyde Walker was giving free tennis lessons once a week. Billie Jean was excited to have a chance to play this new game again. She loved the sound of the racket hitting the ball and the power that made the ball sail back across the net.

After that first lesson with Clyde, Billie Jean knew she had found her sport. She was only ten, but when she got home, she told her mom, "I want to be the number one tennis player in the world!"

CHAPTER 2
Tennis and Life Aren't Fair

Billie Jean was determined to become a better player. She followed everything Clyde Walker taught her about tennis. With the eight dollars and twenty-nine cents she had saved while working odd jobs in her neighborhood, Billie Jean bought her very own wood racket with a grip in her favorite color—purple.

Billie Jean's parents may not have believed that one day their daughter would ever reach the number one spot. But they loved that Billie Jean was willing to work hard to achieve her goal. They encouraged and supported her, and they drove her to coaching sessions and tournaments.

Bill even put up a spotlight in the backyard so that Billie Jean could practice at night.

Billie Jean was learning as much as she could about the game of tennis. And she soon learned being a girl and not being rich meant that things weren't always fair. Tennis was considered a sport that wealthy people played at country clubs. Billie Jean's family was middle-class. They weren't able to afford the expensive equipment and clothing that other kids had. Billie Jean wore clothing and tennis outfits that her mother made.

Boys Billie Jean's age who were good tennis players received a lot more attention from coaches. They often got free meals before or after matches. When Billie Jean was in junior high, her principal refused to sign a permission slip that would allow her to compete in a tournament. She pleaded with the principal, who finally gave in. Billie Jean felt that if she had been a boy, the principal would not have thought twice about signing the permission slip. The mistreatment of someone based on their gender or sex is called sexism.

These things upset Billie Jean, but she didn't let that stop her. She actually became more determined than ever to reach her goal. She also felt that it was her responsibility to help make tennis fairer and more equal. Billie Jean loved the game so much, and she wanted everyone to have an opportunity to play it if they wanted.

Billie Jean's determination and hard work began to pay off. By 1958, she was ranked number two in the age fifteen-and-under Southern California Division. But Billie Jean knew that if she wanted to achieve her dream of being number one in the world, she would need more opportunities to improve her game. Unfortunately, her family couldn't afford the costs of traveling to out-of-state tournaments. So when Billie Jean was offered the opportunity to take lessons with Alice Marble, a former tennis champion, she jumped at the chance.

Billie Jean was thrilled to be coached by a former number one player.

Alice Marble

Alice's stories about her life and tennis matches fascinated Billie Jean, and Alice's coaching made Billie Jean's game get better and better. But Billie Jean and Alice didn't always get along.

Billie Jean thought Alice was arrogant at times, and Alice thought Billie Jean was often selfish and boastful. Eventually, Alice stopped coaching Billie Jean. However, the time Billie Jean spent with Alice paid off. By the middle of 1960, Billie Jean had risen to number four in the rankings of all American female tennis players.

She was proving that her dream of being number one in the world might be possible. However, she still had to deal with people who made sexist remarks and comments about her size. A coach that Billie Jean respected told her that she would be a great tennis player someday. Not because she was a talented athlete—but because she was "ugly." She could spend her time improving her game rather than focusing on boys, clothes, and makeup.

Billie Jean was shocked by this comment. It made her want to work even harder.

The next year, in 1961, Billie Jean had to miss her high school graduation so that she could play doubles (two teams of two players each) with her partner Karen Hantze at Wimbledon. Most people didn't expect Billie Jean and Karen to get very far at the tournament. Everyone, including Billie Jean and Karen, was surprised when they made it to the final championship match—and won.

Wimbledon Ladies' Doubles trophies

Billie Jean and Karen Hantze (left) at Wimbledon, 1961

CHAPTER 3
A Fighter and a Winner

Billie Jean came home a champion, but hardly anyone outside her own family congratulated her on her achievement when she got back to California. On top of that, Billie Jean was sad to learn that while she was in England, her coach Clyde had died. But as always, Billie Jean focused on what was next. And that was heading to college and training to win the women's singles tournament at Wimbledon. In the fall of 1961, Billie Jean began taking classes at Los Angeles State College (now California State University, Los Angeles) and played for the school's tennis team.

At the time, sports scholarships for women didn't exist, so Billie Jean took on part-time jobs to cover her college expenses. Although she was a full-time student, she wasn't always interested in her classes and would rather focus on tennis. She spent a lot of time in the school's library, but she wasn't studying for her classes or exams. Instead, she was reading as much as she could about tennis. She read about the women and men who had become world champions. Billie Jean realized that if she wanted to be number one in the world, then she would need to make training for and playing tennis her main priority.

In the spring of her freshman year, Billie Jean and Karen Hantze went back to Wimbledon and won the doubles championship again. Billie Jean was also playing in the women's singles tournament. In her first match, she beat Margaret Smith, an Australian athlete and the top-ranked women's player in the world at the time.

Margaret Smith

Margaret Smith plays at Wimbledon, 1962

It was the start of a fierce rivalry between the two players. Somewhat surprisingly, Billie Jean lost in the quarterfinals.

Rounds in a Tennis Tournament

In Grand Slam tennis tournaments, 128 players start out playing for the men's and women's singles titles. Once a player has lost a match, they are eliminated. That means there are seven rounds of

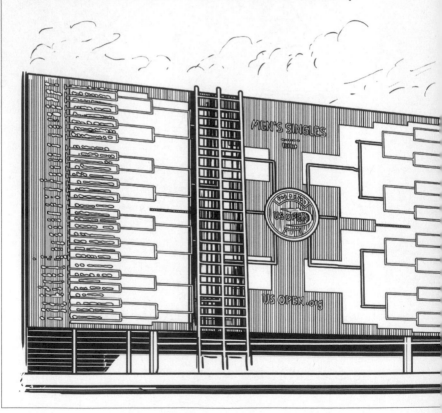

matches from the start of the tournament to the finals. The fifth round, where eight players are left, is called the quarterfinals. The sixth round, where four players are left, is called the semifinals. And the seventh and last round is the finals, where the two remaining players compete for the championship.

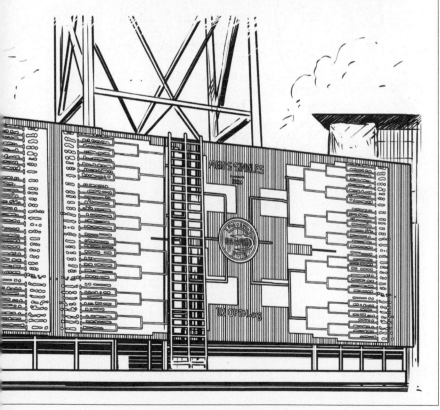

When Billie Jean returned to college for her sophomore year, a friend from the tennis team told her about a freshman she had to meet. Billie Jean wasn't really interested in dating anyone at the time, but her friend still introduced her to the boy, whose name was Larry King. There was something about Larry that Billie Jean was immediately attracted to. He was friendly, sincere, thoughtful, had a great smile—and he played tennis. One of the things that Billie Jean liked most

Larry King

about Larry was his interest in political and social issues. He also had a strong sense of fairness and justice. Billie Jean and Larry began dating, and her feelings for Larry grew even stronger.

One day, Larry told Billie Jean that she was being treated like a second-class citizen just because she was a girl. She asked him what he meant. Larry explained that even though he was probably the worst player on the men's tennis team, he had still received a scholarship to play tennis. But Billie Jean, who was the best athlete at school—among the men—didn't get any financial help. Larry's statement shocked Billie Jean. He was right—there was no reason for her to be treated differently. In fact, there was no reason for any woman to be treated differently than any man in any sport, or in life.

In the summer of 1963, Billie Jean returned to Wimbledon. She made it to the women's singles final, where she played against her rival Margaret Smith. Billie Jean expected to win, but Margaret beat her. The next year, Billie Jean lost to her again in the Wimbledon semifinals.

Margaret Smith wins at Wimbledon, 1963

Billie Jean felt like a failure, but once again, her feelings helped motivate her. Later that year, she was given an opportunity to go to Australia and be coached by Mervyn Rose. He was one of the best tennis coaches in the world . . . and he had been coaching Margaret Smith. Even though it would not be easy and it would mean changing a lot of things, Billie Jean wanted to do it.

While it was going to be difficult to be apart, Larry knew that this was what Billie Jean needed to do. This move to Australia would help her improve her game and move her closer to being number one in the world. Just before Billie Jean left for Australia, Larry proposed to her. He wanted her to know that he loved her, wanted to continue their relationship while she was away, and wanted her to know he would be waiting for her when she returned.

CHAPTER 4
Introducing Billie Jean King

When Billie Jean arrived in Australia, she was ready to do whatever Mervyn asked of her. And he asked a lot. He made Billie Jean change just about everything in the way she played tennis.

He taught her to serve differently, he helped her improve her forehand, and he got her to think more about strategy.

Billie Jean worked with Mervyn for three months. When she arrived back in the United States, she knew she was a better player than when she had left. She was in better shape and ready to compete. Just as exciting for Billie Jean was that she and Larry were together again. They could now start planning their wedding.

It took a while for Billie Jean to start winning matches with her new style of playing. In 1965, she reached the women's singles final of the US National Championships (known as the US Open today). But once again, she lost to Margaret Smith. Afterward, Billie Jean replayed the match in her head, and she realized the difference between her and Margaret. Margaret was able to raise the level of her game when she was under the most pressure. Billie Jean recognized that she had played it too safe in her match with Margaret. Billie Jean would need to be unafraid of taking risks. With that, she could beat anyone.

A few days after that match, on September 17, 1965, Billie Jean and Larry were married. From now on, she would be known as Billie Jean King.

The newlyweds were both still in school. They didn't have a lot of money, so they both had to work. Billie Jean took a job teaching tennis. Larry worked the night shift at an ice cream carton factory. It wasn't easy, but the couple was determined to make their marriage work.

After winning several tournaments in the United States throughout 1965, and because she had reached the women's singles final at the US National Championships, Billie Jean learned she was now ranked the number one women's tennis player in the country! She and Larry agreed that she would leave school and devote all her time to playing tennis. Later on in life, it would bother her that she didn't get to finish her degree, but at the time, she knew playing tennis full-time would bring her one step closer to achieving her dream.

In April 1966, Billie Jean played Margaret Smith at a tournament in South Africa. Her new playing style and attitude had paid off, and she easily beat Margaret. Wimbledon was just a couple of months away, and Billie Jean was convinced that nothing could stop her from winning her first singles title there.

Billie Jean made it to the Wimbledon finals, where her opponent was Brazilian player Maria Bueno. Maria was a three-time Wimbledon champion, and she had beaten Billie Jean many times before. But Billie Jean was determined to win. It wasn't easy but she did it. After winning, she threw her racket high into the air. This was just the beginning.

CHAPTER 5
The Fight Continues

Billie Jean had an even bigger and better year in 1967. That year at Wimbledon, she won the women's singles title, the women's doubles title, and the mixed doubles title. (Mixed doubles is when each team of two players is made up of one woman and one man.)

She also won the women's singles title, along with the women's doubles and mixed doubles titles, at the US National Championships that fall. The last person to do this was her former coach Alice Marble back in 1939.

Winning all those titles meant that Billie Jean was now ranked number one in the world! She had reached the goal she had set for herself when she was ten years old. But even though she was ranked number one in the world, Billie Jean felt many people didn't take her, or women's tennis, seriously. She felt that it was time for her to speak up about the changes she wanted to make. Girls and women weren't given the same opportunities, or paid the same amount of money, as boys and men. And there were hardly any people of color playing tennis. Billie Jean wasn't comfortable giving speeches or talking to crowds, but she knew her number one ranking gave her an opportunity that not many other women would have. Hopefully people would listen to what she had to say.

At the time, the big international tournaments barred professional players; they only allowed amateur athletes to play. (An amateur athlete is someone who does not earn money for playing their sport.) It was thought that amateur athletes were "truer" athletes. They played because they loved the sport, not because they wanted to make money. For example, Billie Jean was now ranked as the best women's player in the world. But she was given just a fourteen-dollar-a-day allowance from tournament organizers. The only way that amateur tennis players were able to survive and make a living was if they came from wealthy families, had a rich spouse, or took money secretly. (Many players were secretly paid by sponsors or organizers so that they could play in certain tournaments.) Billie Jean urged the United States Lawn Tennis Association (USLTA) to let all players, both amateur and professional, play in their tournaments. If they did, then amateur athletes would be able to turn professional, meaning that they would be paid for playing in tournaments.

That way, Billie Jean and other amateur tennis players would take a share of the profits that tournaments made. But the USLTA didn't want to make that change. They felt that "open tennis" would make the game all about making money and not about the love a person has for the sport.

The USLTA threatened to suspend Billie Jean because she spoke out on this issue. But she wasn't going to let the USLTA scare her into being quiet. Billie Jean kept talking about how unfair things were. Finally in 1968, tennis associations were forced to change things because of the criticism they had been receiving from Billie Jean and other tennis players like Roy Emerson and Arthur Ashe.

Billie Jean danced around her apartment when she heard the news. But Larry didn't join her in celebrating. When she asked him why he wasn't excited, he answered, "Just watch, Billie Jean.

Once men get open tennis, they're going to squeeze the women out."

Arthur Ashe and Roy Emerson

Once the open era had begun, Billie Jean and three other female players, along with some male players, decided to turn professional and play for the National Tennis League (NTL). Billie Jean learned that the men in the league were paid almost twice as much as the women players. She wasn't happy about it, but she decided to play.

While playing in the NTL, Billie Jean still took time to play in the traditional tournaments outside of the NTL, like Wimbledon. Billie Jean won the women's singles at Wimbledon in 1968, and her parents were there to watch. It was the first time they had ever seen their daughter play in that tournament.

A wealthy sponsor decided to launch a new tennis league called World Championship Tennis (WCT) in the same year that the NTL was formed. However, the sponsor only wanted men to play in this new league. By 1970, he was offering male players a lot of money, so many of the men left the NTL and moved to the WCT. Billie Jean felt let down. It was just what Larry had predicted.

CHAPTER 6
New Paths

Many of the people in charge of the tennis tournaments were men and former tennis players themselves, and they didn't want to split the prize money equally between the men and women. Numerous tournaments started getting rid of women's matches. Many women players had worked hard to become professionals, but suddenly there were fewer tournaments where they could play at that level.

Billie Jean decided she wasn't going to keep quiet about this problem. She and some other female players came up with a plan. Billie Jean asked Gladys Heldman, the founder and publisher of *World Tennis Magazine*, to talk to the organizer of a large tournament about prize money. But the organizer believed that tennis fans preferred to watch men play and did not want to pay the women. Gladys decided to organize a tournament just for women in Houston that would take place on the same weekend as a big tournament in Los Angeles. The USLTA threatened to ban any women who played in Gladys's tournament, but Gladys and the nine women tennis players who joined her came up with a way around the ban.

Gladys Heldman

Gladys persuaded the tobacco company Philip Morris to fund the tournament with a cigarette brand called Virginia Slims. They would award the winner $2,500 and Gladys contributed $5,000 of her own money, making the total prize $7,500. The USLTA said they would recognize this tournament if it was an amateur event. Billie Jean and the other players were furious. This meant going backward in their fight for equality. But if they rejected the USLTA's demand, how would they be safe from being banned? Gladys had an idea: She would sign up the women to play in her tournament as professionals. So, Billie Jean and the rest of the players signed professional contracts . . . for just one dollar per year.

But the USLTA still banned Billie Jean and her fellow players, and it stripped them of their national rankings. Their decision to play in the new Virginia Slims tournament could have ended their careers, but the women didn't care. It was more important for them to make a point about the unfair treatment of women players. It took a lot of courage for these nine women to make this move. However, they were willing to sacrifice their own careers for the careers of all the other female tennis players. And it was Billie Jean who led the group.

The huge risk paid off. The tournament was such a big success that Philip Morris agreed to fund a series of tournaments. It was the beginning of the Virginia Slims Circuit that lasted for two years and was replaced with the Women's Tennis Association (WTA) Tour. This association was developed by Billie Jean.

Billie Jean after winning the Virginia Slims
women's tournament in 1971

Even though the women playing in the Virginia Slims tour had broken off from the USLTA, many of the top-ranked women continued to play for them, including a new star named Chris Evert.

Chris Evert plays against Billie Jean, 1971

Larry was thrilled that Billie Jean had made the Virginia Slims tour happen. But it meant that the two of them were spending less and less time together. Billie Jean was traveling around the country on the tour, while Larry was working hard at his job. After graduating from law school, he started a company to help promote Billie Jean's tournaments. The couple never seemed to be in the same city at the same time.

While Billie Jean and Larry still loved and respected each other, they realized they were drifting apart.

Billie Jean also started thinking that she might be as attracted to women as she was to Larry. She knew that she loved Larry. He supported her and wanted her to succeed just as much as she did. But Billie Jean wasn't sure that their relationship made her happy. She was struggling with how she felt about Larry, who she was, and what she wanted to be. And she was thinking that might include having romantic feelings toward women. Billie Jean and Larry didn't have time to talk about their relationship or Billie Jean's developing feelings because they were both focused on building successful careers.

The Virginia Slims tour introduced the game of tennis to lots of new fans. It proved that women's sports were popular. One of the people who became very interested in the success of the Virginia Slims tournament was the man who had won the men's singles championship at Wimbledon in 1939. His name was Bobby Riggs.

Bobby Riggs

CHAPTER 7
The Battle of the Sexes

Bobby Riggs had been a top tennis player in the 1930s and 1940s. But now he was over fifty years old, and he no longer earned money by playing in tournaments. The way he made

Bobby Riggs wins the national professional
tennis championship, 1946

money was by challenging younger players to competitions. And as soon as Bobby and Billie Jean met in 1971, he started asking her to play against him. At that time, the term *chauvinist pig* was used to describe a man who felt women weren't as intelligent or as deserving of respect as men. *Chauvinist* is a word that refers to a person who thinks they are better than others. And Bobby was happy to call himself that term. He thought men were superior to women, and he wanted to prove his point by playing, and beating, a top women's tennis player.

Billie Jean didn't want to play Bobby. She felt that if she won, people would say "big deal."

But if she lost, then people would believe that all women couldn't play tennis as well as men. And that would mean women didn't deserve to play in the same number of tournaments a year, earn the same amount of money, and get the same amount of television coverage as men.

Throughout 1971 and 1972, Billie Jean continued winning tournaments. She became the first woman professional athlete in any sport to earn $100,000 in a year.

In December 1972, *Sports Illustrated* magazine put Billie Jean on the cover as its "Sportswoman of the Year." It was the first time the magazine had ever honored a woman in this way. The honor was for how Billie Jean played on the tennis court and the way she fought for women's rights while off the tennis court.

During the late 1960s and early 1970s, the women's rights movement made great progress in gaining more personal and political freedoms for women. Billie Jean helped lead the fight, and she stood up and spoke out for women athletes and women everywhere.

Title IX

Up until the early 1970s, women and girls didn't have the same opportunities as men and boys to play on sports teams. That's because high schools and colleges spent money mainly on the men's and boys' teams. (For example, in 1969, one college budgeted $90,000 for men's sports—and only $200 for women's.) The training programs, locker rooms, and equipment for female students were usually not as good as what the male students had.

But in 1972, Title IX of the Education Amendments was passed by Congress. It was signed into law by President Richard Nixon on June 23, 1972. It was now the law that schools that received federal funding, such as public high schools and colleges, had to provide equal sports programs for girls and boys.

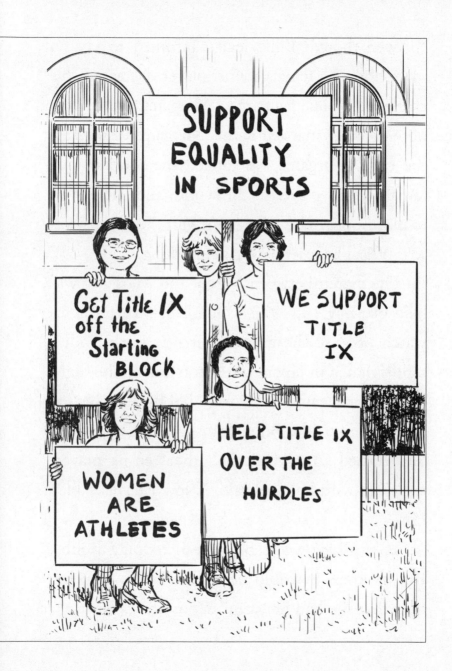

Even though Billie Jean continued to say no to Bobby, one female tennis player did accept his challenge—Billie Jean's rival, Margaret Smith. (She now used her married name, Margaret Court.) At the time, Margaret was ranked the number one female tennis player in the world, and she agreed to play Bobby. The prize money for the winner was $10,000. The loser would get nothing.

The match between Bobby and Margaret was held on May 13, 1973. Billie Jean wasn't able to watch because she was on her way back from a tennis match in Japan. On a stop during the flight home, she heard the score—Bobby had beaten Margaret quickly. Billie Jean couldn't believe it. She turned to one of the other tennis players traveling with her and said, "Now I have to play him."

Larry didn't want Billie Jean to play Bobby. But he knew it would be impossible to stop her now that she had her mind set on it.

Bobby Riggs and Margaret Court

As soon as the match was announced, it was talked about on television programs and in newspapers. And it had been given the name the "Battle of the Sexes."

The match would be played on September 20, 1973, at the Astrodome, a huge sports stadium in Houston, Texas. In the weeks leading up to the match, Billie Jean prepared as much as she could. She learned that the stadium had a white roof. It would be difficult to see the tennis ball when it was up in the air and close to the stadium lights. She knew that Bobby liked to hit balls high into the air. So Billie Jean practiced hitting hundreds of overhead shots every day.

Bobby, on the other hand, didn't practice very much at all. He had beaten Margaret Court, and he figured it would be even easier to beat Billie Jean.

The Battle of the Sexes was not like a regular tennis match. There were cheerleaders, bands, and balloons. All this hype and excitement was making Billie Jean nervous, but she stayed focused. Bobby was playing to make money and promote himself. She was playing for women's equality.

Billie Jean had insisted that she and Bobby play best three out of five sets (like the professional men played) just to prove that women were as good as men. Billie Jean didn't hold back, and she made Bobby run for every shot.

After only three games in the first set, Bobby was covered in sweat and breathing heavily.

Just as Billie Jean had suspected, Bobby hit a lot of shots high overhead. But she was ready and didn't miss a single overhead shot. She also hit to Bobby's backhand, which Margaret Court had told her was his weakness. As the match went on,

Bobby got very tired, but Billie Jean became
energized. The crowd in the Astrodome started
to feel sorry for Bobby. Fans who supported him

cheered him on, but that didn't help. Billie Jean
won the first set 6–4 and the second set 6–3. If
she won one more set, she would win the match.

Bobby Riggs was no longer laughing or boasting. And when he hit a shot into the net to end the match, everyone knew he had just lost the Battle of the Sexes. Billie Jean threw her racket into the air and gave a huge smile. The crowd rushed onto the court. Bobby had just enough energy left to jump over the net to congratulate Billie Jean. "You're too good," he said. "I underestimated you."

Billie Jean's victory was celebrated by women around the world. For many, it was the first time they had seen a woman beat a man at anything. At the press conference after the match, Billie Jean said, "This is the culmination of nineteen years of work. . . . I've wanted to change the game around. Now it's here."

CHAPTER 8
Facing Challenges

On the night of the Battle of the Sexes competition, a woman sat next to Billie Jean during breaks in the match. Her name was Marilyn Barnett. Billie Jean and Marilyn had met in the spring of 1972. She had started out as Billie Jean's hairdresser, but she and Billie Jean soon became good friends. Marilyn was not involved in the world of sports, and it was easy for Billie Jean to relax and be herself around Marilyn, so she hired her to be her personal assistant. Marilyn accompanied

Marilyn Barnett

Billie Jean to her matches and helped organize her busy schedule.

Billie Jean soon started dating Marilyn secretly and realized she was falling in love with her. Billie Jean already knew she could have romantic feelings for women, but she wasn't sure what to do because she was still married to Larry. Marilyn often pressured Billie Jean to reveal their relationship. But Billie Jean knew that telling people she was in love with a woman could ruin her career. At the time, same-sex couples were not common, and many people were homophobic, meaning they had a fear, mistrust, or even hatred of people who are gay. *Gay* is a word used to describe people who have romantic attraction and feelings for people of the same sex.

To get away from the stress in her personal life, Billie Jean focused on what she could do for women tennis players. Now that she was an international celebrity, people were willing to listen to and work with her more than ever. Billie Jean testified before Congress—the part of the United States government that makes laws—to talk about the Women's Educational Equity Act. This act, passed in 1974, created federal grants that helped schools fund the things that were required by Title IX. A grant is an award of money given by a government or organization for a specific purpose. Billie Jean helped create the Women's Sports Foundation, an organization that worked to give women and girls in America more opportunities in sports. She also helped get *womenSports* started. It was a magazine dedicated to women and girls in sports.

Even though she was involved in a lot of other things, Billie Jean also continued to play and win several tennis tournaments. In 1975, she started to think about retiring. She was only in her early thirties, but she was older than many of the players she faced on the court. And Billie Jean felt it would be better to retire when she was still playing very well. She decided that she would continue to play doubles, but Wimbledon in 1975 would be her final singles tournament. Billie Jean won—it was a great way to retire. After the match, she told the press, "I'm never coming back." At first Billie Jean enjoyed being retired. She could stay up late, eat whatever she wanted, and relax on the beach. She and Larry had thought that her retirement would bring the two of them closer together, but it was too late for that. Billie Jean and Larry had grown even further apart, and she was still in a relationship with Marilyn.

Equal Rights for Everyone?

For centuries, being gay was a crime in America. And it is still considered a crime in many other countries. If someone was discovered to be in a same-sex relationship or to have feelings for someone of the same sex, they could lose their job, be sent to prison, or get sentenced to death. Things began to change in the United States on June 28, 1969, when a group of brave queer people at the Stonewall Inn bar in New York City fought against police officers who were harassing them. (*Queer* is a term that is often used to describe people who are not strictly attracted to people of the opposite sex.) These actions encouraged the queer community to speak up and try to change the unfair laws that targeted them. By 2003, many states had removed laws that discriminated against queer people, and by 2015, it was a federal crime to harm someone just because they are queer, and the Supreme Court ruled that same-sex couples have the same legal right to marry as different-sex couples.

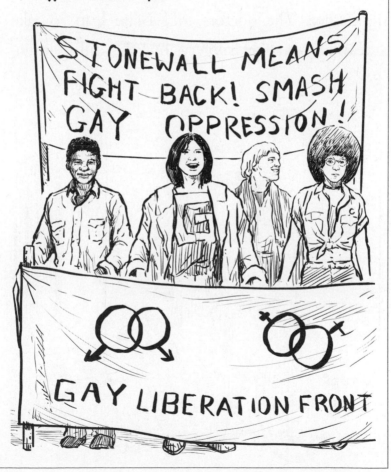

After a while, Billie Jean discovered that she missed the excitement of tennis tournaments and playing in front of fans. In 1977, she decided to come out of retirement and get back on the tour. But first she would need to have surgery to fix her right knee. The doctors told Billie Jean to take a year off after her surgery, but she didn't listen.

After only six months, she was playing at Wimbledon. Although she lost to Chris Evert in the quarterfinals, Billie Jean wasn't upset. "Maybe I can be happy being number eight instead of number one," she told a reporter.

In 1978, Billie Jean didn't win any major tournaments in singles or doubles. But in 1979, she broke the record for the most wins at Wimbledon when she and her doubles partner, Martina Navratilova, won the title.

Martina Navratilova

Billie Jean and Martina also won the doubles title at the US Open in 1980.

Another one of Billie Jean's doubles partners was Ilana Kloss, a younger player from South Africa. Billie Jean had met Ilana years earlier, and she admired how honest and caring Ilana was.

Ilana Kloss (left) with Billie Jean

Billie Jean also loved that fairness and justice were just as important to Ilana as they were to her. And now Billie Jean found herself having strong romantic feelings for Ilana. Billie Jean, who was no longer seeing Marilyn Barnett but was still married to Larry, wasn't sure what to do with the relationships in her life.

In the spring of 1981, Marilyn filed a lawsuit against Billie Jean and claimed that Billie Jean owed her half of all the money she had won while they were together. Marilyn also said she was owed the house in California where the two had spent time together.

Marilyn's lawsuit made it clear she and Billie Jean had had a romantic relationship. The most private part of Billie Jean's life had been revealed. What would Billie Jean's family think? How would her fans react? What would her friends say? Billie Jean was scared.

CHAPTER 9
Looking Forward

At first Billie Jean denied Marilyn Barnett's claims. But Marilyn had love letters that Billie Jean had written to her over the years, and she was willing to share them with news reporters. Billie Jean knew she had to tell the truth, but she was worried that people would not accept her for who she was.

On May 1, 1981, Billie Jean held a press conference and announced that she had dated Marilyn. She had stood up for women's rights, and

now she was standing up for the rights of gay people.

A judge dismissed Marilyn's case and

stated that what Marilyn had done was an attempt at extortion. (Extortion is when you force someone to give you something, usually money, through threats.)

Marilyn Barnett talks to press after 1981 lawsuit case

Billie Jean and Larry stayed together during the lawsuit with Marilyn. He even sat next to Billie Jean at her press conference. However, in 1987, the couple no longer thought it was

right to remain married, so they got divorced. Billie Jean and Larry were sad, but they knew separating would allow them to find people who made them happier. And for Billie Jean, the person who made her happiest was Ilana Kloss.

Billie Jean continued to play tennis after the lawsuit was dropped, but she lost several matches early on in some tournaments, and she even walked off the court during one match. Billie Jean was upset, but she had made up her mind to not let what happened in her personal life affect her game. She reached the semifinals at Wimbledon in 1982 and 1983 and stayed a top-twenty-ranking player both years.

However, because of her relationship with Marilyn, many of the companies that endorsed Billie Jean withdrew their support. She lost close to $1.5 million in deals with big-name companies over the next three years. Even though these deals were gone, Billie Jean received a lot of support from other tennis players. And she also received thousands of letters from fans, praising her for her honesty and bravery.

In 1984, when Billie Jean was forty years old, she decided it was finally time to retire for good. But even though she would no longer be playing tennis, she knew there was still more she could do to get women sports players the recognition and money they deserved. In 1987, Billie Jean was celebrated for being one of the world's greatest tennis players when she was inducted into the International Tennis Hall of Fame.

Billie Jean began helping female tennis players by coaching them. Martina Navratilova, one of Billie Jean's former doubles partners, had been the top women's player in the 1980s. But by 1989, she was losing matches, and she hadn't won a Grand Slam in two years. With Billie Jean's coaching, Martina went on to win her record ninth Wimbledon singles title in 1990. She said it was thanks to Billie Jean that she rediscovered her love for the game of tennis.

Billie Jean loved this newfound career as a

coach. She not only coached players one-on-one, but she also took over as captain of the US Federation Cup Team in 1995. And she coached the US Women's Olympic tennis teams in 1996 and 2000. Those teams won gold medals in both the singles and doubles matches. The young women who played on those Olympic teams (including Venus and Serena Williams) were the first generation of female tennis players who benefited from the work Billie Jean had done.

US Federation Cup Team in 1999

Billie Jean's demands gave these women equal opportunities, better prize money, and more TV coverage. According to ESPN, a sports network, the women's championship match at the US Open in 2021 attracted an average of 17 percent more viewers than the men's match.

CHAPTER 10
The Work Never Stops

Billie Jean had accomplished a lot in her professional career, but she wasn't happy with the personal side of her life. Even though she was now fifty-one years old, she had never felt comfortable enough to tell her parents that she was gay. She worried they would be upset, but she no longer wanted to hide her relationship with Ilana from her family. Coming out to her parents was the hardest thing Billie Jean had ever done.

But she said that once she did it, she felt more at peace with herself and her life than ever before.

In 2006, Billie Jean's dedication to tennis was rewarded in a very special way. The National Tennis Center would be renamed the USTA Billie Jean King National Tennis Center. (In 1975, the USLTA dropped the word "Lawn" from its name, and it became the USTA.)

Billie Jean couldn't believe it! Not only was the USTA going to name the center after a woman, but also after someone who had fought them about equal opportunities for everyone. It was a real sign that things had changed. When she gave a speech at the rededication ceremony for the center, Billie Jean said, "*Mi casa es su casa.* My house is your house! This is *our* house."

In 2009, President Barack Obama presented Billie Jean with the Presidential Medal of Freedom.

It is the highest award given to civilians in the United States. Billie Jean received this medal for her extraordinary achievements in tennis, both as a player and a promoter of equal rights for women. This was the first time the medal had been awarded to a woman athlete.

Having a national tennis center named after her and receiving a presidential medal didn't mean that Billie Jean slowed down at all. She continues to promote the sport she loves and fight for equality not only in sports but in every part

BILLIE JEAN KING
Leadership Initiative
Lift. Learn. Lead.

of society. To help achieve that goal, in 2014 Billie Jean and Ilana founded the Billie Jean King Leadership Initiative. The organization works to ensure that all employees have equal opportunities and rights in their workplaces. Billie Jean also speaks at protests and marches that fight for equal rights for all.

In 2017, forty-four years after the historic event, a feature film was made about the Battle of the Sexes. It starred Emma Stone as Billie Jean King and Steve Carell as Bobby Riggs.

The USTA Billie Jean King National Tennis Center

Located in Queens, New York, the USTA Billie Jean King National Tennis Center is one of the world's largest public tennis facilities. It is home to the US Open tennis tournament, which takes place there for two weeks every August and September.

The center was originally built in 1978, but more courts and tennis stadiums were added over the years. The main tennis court is named after Arthur Ashe, the first Black man to win a Grand Slam title.

By 2018, Billie Jean and Ilana had been in a serious relationship for almost forty years. But Billie Jean wanted to make sure Ilana knew just how much she trusted and loved her, so the couple decided to make their commitment to each other legal by getting married. They didn't want a big, fancy wedding, though. Billie Jean wore a tracksuit!

Billie Jean and Ilana in 2018

Three years later, Billie Jean was honored with the Sports Illustrated Muhammad Ali Legacy Award. The award is given to an athlete who best represents the ideals of sportsmanship, leadership, and philanthropy as ways to change the world. (Philanthropy is the practice of giving money and time to help make life better for other people.) In 2021, Billie Jean also published her autobiography, *All In*. She had written several other books about her life, but she used this book to finally speak about the struggles she had experienced in her life and how she finally came to be happy with herself. The book showed the world that throughout her life, starting when she was just

a young girl, Billie Jean has pushed for positive change, not only in tennis but across society.

Timeline of Billie Jean King's Life

1943 — Billie Jean Moffitt is born in Long Beach, California, on November 22

1954 — Takes her first tennis lesson

1961 — Wins Wimbledon women's doubles championship with Karen Hantze

1964 — Spends three months in Australia working with coach and tennis player Mervyn Rose

1965 — Marries Larry King on September 17

1966 — Wins first Wimbledon women's singles title

1970 — Helps organize the Virginia Slims tour

1972 — Begins a relationship with Marilyn Barnett

1973 — Defeats Bobby Riggs in the Battle of the Sexes on September 20

1981 — Marilyn Barnett files a lawsuit that exposes her romantic relationship with Billie Jean

1984 — Retires from playing tennis at age forty

1987 — Divorces Larry; elected to the International Tennis Hall of Fame

2006 — National Tennis Center is renamed after Billie Jean

2009 — Receives Presidential Medal of Freedom

2018 — Marries Ilana Kloss

2021 — Publishes autobiography *All In*

Timeline of the World

1945	Atomic bombs are dropped on the cities Hiroshima and Nagasaki in Japan, ending World War II
1947	Jackie Robinson becomes the first Black player to join a major league baseball team in the United States
1955	Polio vaccine is introduced
1963	United States president John F. Kennedy is assassinated
1969	Woodstock Music Festival takes place in New York State
1974	Girls allowed to play in Little League Baseball programs in the United States
1976	Apple Computer company launches
1983	Sally Ride becomes the first American woman in space
1989	The Berlin Wall that separated West and East Germany after World War II is torn down
2001	The World Trade Center buildings in New York City are attacked by terrorists
2008	Barack Obama is elected president of the United States
2014	Teen activist Malala Yousafzai wins the Nobel Peace Prize for her work in equal education for all children
2021	Due to the COVID-19 pandemic, the 2020 Summer Olympics are rescheduled and held in Japan

Bibliography

*Books for young readers

*Gitlin, Marty. *Billie Jean King: Tennis Star & Social Activist*. Edina, MN: ABDO Publishing Company, 2011.

King, Billie Jean. *All In: An Autobiography*. New York: Alfred A. Knopf, 2021.

*Lannin, Joanne. *Billie Jean King: Tennis Trailblazer*. Minneapolis, MN: Lerner Publications Company, 1999.

*Meltzer, Brad. *I am Billie Jean King*. New York: Dial Books for Young Readers, 2019.

*Rockliff, Mara. *Billie Jean! How Tennis Star Billie Jean King Changed Women's Sports*. New York: G. P. Putnam's Sons, 2019.

*Sánchez Vegara, Maria Isabel. *Little People, Big Dreams: Billie Jean King*. London: Frances Lincoln Children's Books, 2020.

Ware, Susan. *Game, Set, Match: Billie Jean King and the Revolution in Women's Sports*. Chapel Hill, NC: The University of North Carolina Press, 2011.